THE OFFICIAL 2016
BORO ANNUAL

CW00671463

This book belongs to

Age

Favourite player

Prediction of Middlesbrough's final position this season

Prediction of Sky Bet Championship winners this season

Prediction of FA Cup winners this season

Prediction of Capital One Cup winners this season

Prediction of teams to be relegated
from the Sky Bet Championship this season:

22nd

23rd

24th

Written by twocan

Contributors:
Graham Bell & Rob Mason

A TWOCAN PUBLICATION

©2015. Published by twocan under licence from Middlesbrough FC.

ISBN 978-1-909872-43-1

£8

Contents

Fitness first

Footballers are getting fitter and fitter. Just as athletics records are broken, as runners get faster and faster, in football each generation of players are faster, fitter and stronger than before.

Clubs have more and more support staff to provide everything a player will need to help him become the supreme athlete. These days, teams have fitness & conditioning coaches and nutritionists, who make sure every player is in the best physical shape he can be.

In pre-season, clubs carry out all kinds of tests on their players to monitor their progress and ensure each individual reaches and maintains peak fitness. A lot of work is done in the gym with weights, designed to make sure players have the strength not to be easily knocked off the ball and that they also possess the stamina to get through 90 minutes and not fade in the game's latter stages.

Of course, while fitness is essential, ultimately it is their ability that matters. Footballers like to train with the ball and work hard on their skills. A lot of drills are undertaken to develop and maintain each player's ability on the ball. Coaching staff also work on team play, formations and developing understandings on the pitch.

A large proportion of goals come from set-pieces so teams work on not just taking them, but defending free-kicks, corners and throw-ins. Every team has a specialist dead-ball expert who they rely on for these important moments in games. Some teams prefer to do man-for-man marking and some use the zonal approach. In man-for-man marking, every player has a responsibility to mark a particular opponent, while zonal marking means every player has an area of the pitch that they have to defend.

Whichever system is used, it is important that players work hard in training, so that they are a fully fit and well organised unit and can perform together successfully as a team.

The Squad

Dimitrios
KONSTANTOPOULOS
01

Position: Goalkeeper **Nationality:** Greek **DOB:** 29th November 1978
Height: 6'4" (193cm) **Weight:** 14st 11lbs (94kg)

Boro signed experienced Greek shot-stopper Dimi, in August 2013 on a short-term contract which was later extended. He has been capped once at full international level for Greece, and has also won nine U21 caps.

George
FRIEND
03

Position: Defender **Nationality:** English **DOB:** 17th October 1987
Height: 6'2" (188cm) **Weight:** 13st 5lbs (85kg)

One of Boro's most popular players on and off the field, Friend was named in the PFA Championship Team of the Year following an impressive 2014/15 season and was also named vice-captain this season.

Abella
DAMIA
02

Position: Defender **Nationality:** Spanish **DOB:** 15th April 1982
Height: 6'2" (188cm) **Weight:** 13st 5lbs (85kg)

In August 2014 Damia signed for Boro on a free transfer from Osasuna and made his debut against Leeds United at Elland Road. An experienced full-back, he has played for the likes of Barcelona and Real Betis.

Daniel AYALA 04

Position: Defender Nationality: Spanish DOB: 7th November 1990
Height: 6'3" (190cm) Weight: 14st 0lbs (89kg)

Ayala initially joined Boro on a 93-day emergency loan from Norwich City in October 2013 but signed a permanent deal in January 2014. He scored with a towering header on his debut in the 4-0 win over Doncaster Rovers at the Riverside.

Fernando AMOREBIETA 05

Position: Defender Nationality: Venezuelan DOB: 29th March 1985
Height: 6'3" (190cm) Weight: 13st 7lbs (87kg)

Amorebieta joined Boro on a season-long loan from Fulham this August. He has spent most of his pro career with Athletic Bilbao, appearing in over 250 games over the course of eight La Liga seasons.

Ben GIBSON 06

Position: Defender Nationality: English DOB: 15th January 1993
Height: 6'1" (185cm) Weight: 13st 5lbs (85kg)

Gibson turned professional in July 2010 as one of six Academy players handed their first pro contracts. Equally at home at left-back or in central defence, he has made winning trophies a good habit early in his career for both club and country.

Adam CLAYTON
08

Position: Midfielder   Nationality: English   DOB: 14th January 1989
Height: 5'9" (175cm)   Weight: 12st 4lbs (78kg)

Clayton is a product of the Manchester City Academy where he signed at the age of seven. He joined Middlesbrough on a four-year deal in August 2014 and firmly established himself as a regular last season.

Grant LEADBITTER
07

Position: Midfielder   Nationality: English   DOB: 7th January 1986
Height: 5'10" (177cm)   Weight: 12st 4lbs (78kg)

Leadbitter agreed a three-year contract extension in December 2014. His consistent performances and selection of incredible goals led to him being named in the PFA Championship Team of the Year last season.

KIKE
09

Position: Striker   Nationality: Spanish   DOB: 25th November 1989
Height: 6'1" (186cm)   Weight: 13st 7lbs (86.2kg)

Brought in as Aitor Karanka's primary summer target for the 2014/15 season, Kike has represented his nation at U20s level. On 15 August 2015, he scored his first brace for Boro, in the 3-0 win against Bolton Wanderers.

Tomas
MEJIAS
13

Position: Goalkeeper **Nationality:** Spanish **DOB:** 30th January 1989
Height: 6'5" (195cm) **Weight:** 13st 12lbs (88kg)

A product of Real Madrid's youth system, Mejias had spent his whole professional career with the Spanish outfit until moving to Boro permanently in July 2014 after a loan spell. He has also made appearances for the Spain U19 and U20 sides.

Carlos
DE PENA
10

Position: Midfielder **Nationality:** Uruguayan **DOB:** 11th March 1992
Height: 5'10" (177cm) **Weight:** 11st 2lbs (71kg)

De Pena started his pro career at Montevideo-based Nacional, where he made 53 appearances and scored 10 goals before moving to Boro this summer. He is the second Uruguayan signing of the season, joining striker Cristhian Stuani.

Rhys
WILLIAMS
14

Position: Defender **Nationality:** Australian **DOB:** 14th July 1988
Height: 6'2" (186.7cm) **Weight:** 12st 6lbs (79kg)

A versatile defender who can also perform in a central midfield role, Williams has suffered with injuries recently and only managed two appearances last season. He has represented Australia at international level on a number of occasions.

Alex
BAPTISTE
15

Position: Defender   **Nationality:** English   **DOB:** 31st January 1986
Height: 5'11" (180.3cm)   **Weight:** 12st 4lbs (78kg)

A versatile defender who can play anywhere in the back four, Baptiste joined the squad on a three-year contract in July 2015. He has clocked up over 300 career appearances, notably at Mansfield Town and Blackpool.

Jack
STEPHENS
16

Position: Defender   **Nationality:** English   **DOB:** 27th January 1994
Height: 6'1" (185cm)   **Weight:** 12st 12lbs (82kg)

A versatile defender, Stephens joined Boro on a season-long loan from Southampton in August 2015. He enjoyed a successful campaign last season and made 41 appearances on loan at Swindon Town.

Cristhian
STUANI
18

Position: Striker   **Nationality:** Uruguayan   **DOB:** 12th October 1986
Height: 6'0" (184cm)   **Weight:** 12st 6lbs (79kg)

Stuani joined Boro in August 2015 from Espanyol, where he had scored 15 goals in 47 appearances in the 2014/15 season. He has so far made over 20 international appearances for Uruguay.

Adam REACH 20

Position: Midfielder   Nationality: English   DOB: 3rd February 1993
Height: 6'1" (185cm)   Weight: 12st 12lbs (82kg)

A tall, quick, left-sided player, Reach was elevated to the first team squad after impressive displays in the FA Youth Cup and for the Reserves during the 2010/11 campaign. He has now firmly established himself as a regular.

Stewart DOWNING 19

Position: Midfielder   Nationality: English   DOB: 22nd July 1984
Height: 5'11" (180.3cm)   Weight: 12st 4lbs (78kg)

A product of the Boro Academy, Downing completed his move back to Boro from West Ham in July 2015. He boasts 35 England caps and has made over 500 career appearances at the highest level, and has scored 50 goals.

Dael FRY 22

Position: Defender   Nationality: English
DOB: 30th August 1997

Fry started at the age of five for Cleveland Juniors and was scouted by Boro at the age of nine. A tall centre-half who loves defending, he is also a big threat from set pieces. He has represented England at U17 level.

Michael AGAZZI

25

Position: Goalkeeper   Nationality: Italian
DOB: 3rd July 1984

Agazzi joined Boro on loan from AC Milan this August. He has played for a number of clubs, most notably Cagliari, where he established himself firmly as first choice keeper, making well over 100 appearances for the club.

Emilio NSUE

24

Position: Midfielder   Nationality: Equatoguinean   DOB: 30th September 1989
Height: 5'10" (178cm)   Weight: 12st 2lbs (77kg)

Nsue moved to Boro in July 2014 after his contract at Mallorca ended. He is a versatile player who can do a job on the right side of midfield, up front or even at right-back if needed.

Tomas KALAS

26

Position: Defender   Nationality: Czech   DOB: 15th May 1993
Height: 6'0" (184cm)   Weight: 12st 4lbs (78kg)

Kalas arrived on Teesside for a second loan spell from Chelsea that will keep him at Boro until the end of the season. The versatile 22-year-old can play at either right-back or centre-back.

Albert ADOMAH 27

Position: Midfielder **Nationality:** Ghanaian **DOB:** 13th December 1987
Height: 6'0" (182cm) **Weight:** 11st 9lbs (74kg)

An exciting Ghanaian international, Adomah joined Boro from Bristol City for an undisclosed fee in August 2013, on a three-year contract. He was named in Ghana's squad for the World Cup finals in Brazil and played in two games.

Yanic WILDSCHUT 30

Position: Midfielder **Nationality:** Dutch **DOB:** 1st November 1991
Height: 6'2" (187cm) **Weight:** 14st 2lbs (90kg)

A product of the famous Ajax Academy, Wildschut joined Boro in September 2014 on a two-year contract. The pacey winger has took in spells at FC Zwolle, VVV-Venlo, SC Heerenveen and ADO Den Haag.

Diego FABBRINI 31

Position: Striker **Nationality:** Italian **DOB:** 31st July 1990
Height: 5'11" (181cm) **Weight:** 10st 10lbs (68kg)

Fabbrini joined Boro from Watford on a season-long loan in July 2015. He spent the majority of last season on loan at Millwall and Birmingham where he picked up valuable Championship experience.

Adam
FORSHAW
34

Position: Midfielder   **Nationality:** English   **DOB:** 8th October 1991
Height: 6'1" (185.4cm)   **Weight:** 11st 13lbs (76kg)

Forshaw is a product of the Everton Academy and stayed at Goodison Park until 2012. He joined Middlesbrough in January 2015 on a three-and-a-half-year contract and made 20 appearances over the second half of the season.

David
NUGENT
35

Position: Striker   **Nationality:** English   **DOB:** 2nd May 1985
Height: 5'11" (180.3cm)   **Weight:** 13st 5lbs (85kg)

Nugent signed for Boro from Leicester City in August 2015 on a three-year deal. He has previously played for Bury, Preston, Portsmouth and Burnley before joining Leicester in 2011. He also has one cap for England.

Mark
KITCHING
37

Position: Defender   **Nationality:** English
DOB: 4th September 1995

Classy Mark can operate in either defence or midfield. He was a Boro Season Card holder and describes himself as a true fan. After breaking into the first team late in 2013/14, he was awarded a pro contract at the end of the season.

Jonathan
WOODGATE
39

Position: Defender   **Nationality:** English   **DOB:** 22nd January 1980
Height: 6'0" (182.8cm)   **Weight:** 13st 3lbs (84kg)

Woodgate returned to his hometown club after agreeing a three-year contract in July 2012 and signed a one-year extension this July. He is a former England international with eight full caps to his name.

Andre
BENNETT

Position: Defender **Nationality:** English **DOB:** 22nd October 1994
Height: 5'8" (173cm) **Weight:** 10st 3lbs (65kg)

Andre Bennett is a versatile midfielder or defender. He broke into Boro's U21 side early in the 2012/13 season and was drafted into the first team squad in January 2013.

Bradley
FEWSTER

Position: Striker **Nationality:** English **DOB:** 27th January 1996
Height: 5'10" (178cm) **Weight:** 11st 11lbs (75kg)

An England U19 international, Fewster successfully broke into Boro's U21 team during the 2012/13 season, scoring several vital goals. His progress was rewarded with a three-year professional contract in summer 2013.

Jordan
JONES

Position: Midfielder **Nationality:** English **DOB:** 24th October 1994
Height: 5'9" (174cm) **Weight:** 10st 3lbs (65kg)

Born in Middlesbrough, Jones is described by Dave Parnaby as a 'very exciting, individual-type of player'. He made his first team debut as a substitute in the 4-1 FA Cup third round win over Hastings in January 2013.

Adam
JACKSON

Position: Defender **Nationality:** English
DOB: 18th May 1994

Darlington-born Jackson is a classy central defender of whom big things are hoped. He was a key member of the Boro squad that reached the FA Youth Cup quarter-finals in 2011 and has also represented England at youth level.

Test Yourself on 2015
Middlesbrough FC

How much do you know about Middlesbrough's last year?

Take our test and find out!

01

Who was Boro's top League goal scorer last season and how many did he score?

02

Who scored Boro's final goal of the 2014/15 season in the 3-0 victory at home to Brentford?

03

Which former Bolton Wanderers player was first to be signed to Middlesbrough this summer on a free transfer?

04

In which month was Aitor Karanka named Manager of the Month last season?

05

Who were Boro's joint three top appearance makers last season and how many appearances did they each make across all competitions?

06

Striker Cristhian Stuani is now a permanent member of the MFC squad since he switched from Espanyol in the summer. Which international team has he represented?

07

Who has come in on loan from AC Milan until the end of the season?

08

Boro had the highest attendance of 33,381 in the Championship last term. Who were they playing?

09

This summer, Boro re-signed a midfielder who started his career with the MFC Academy. Who is he?

10

Which Boro player has gone out on loan to Huddersfield Town until the end of the 2015/16 season?

11

Who are Boro playing in their last game of 2015?

12

Against whom was Boro's first League win of the calendar year?

13

Who scored the first League goal for Boro this season?

14

Midfielder, Grant Leadbitter is Boro's acting captain this season. How many goals did he score last season?

15

David Nugent signed for Boro this August from Leicester City. Who did he score his first Boro goal against this September?

ANSWERS ON PAGE 62

19

Spot the Difference

Can you spot the eight differences between these two celebration shots?

Stewart DOWNING

The Second Half
OF THE 2014/15 SEASON

Christmas is always a good moment to take stock and try to work out where clubs will finish at the end of the season. Boro were fourth at the turn of the year – and that is the position they occupied after the final Sky Bet Championship match with Brighton on 2 May.

There were all sorts of twists and turns ahead, of course, but none of Boro's rivals took a stranglehold on the league in one of the most exciting promotion campaigns for many years. What added extra spice to Boro's post-Christmas programme was a thrilling FA Cup run.

Few neutrals gave Aitor Karanka's players much chance when they were drawn against the reigning Premier League champions Manchester City at the Etihad Stadium in the fourth round. But Boro turned on the style on a day of upsets for the big boys.

It was a match that had everything, with Patrick Bamford and substitute Kike scoring the goals that dumped City out of the competition. Keeper Tomas Mejias was in inspired form to keep the home side out in the first half and the result sent shockwaves through football.

Back in the league, Boro kept up the momentum by claiming some big results. Wins at Derby County and Norwich City kept them firmly in the promotion pack, but defeats to main rivals Bournemouth and Watford ultimately proved vital.

Fourth place brought the play-offs, and what a start they made with stirring victories over Brentford in the semi-finals. But Norwich ended the dream at Wembley, their 2-0 win restoring their Premier League status at the first time of asking.

Boro, however, had come agonisingly close to knocking Liverpool out of the Capital One Cup back in September, only losing to the Champions League qualifiers at Anfield after one of the longest penalty shoot-outs in history.

They faced another of the Premier League's elite in the FA Cup fifth round when then they travelled to Arsenal. The Gunners triumphed 2-0 to end Boro's impressive progress.

CULT heroes

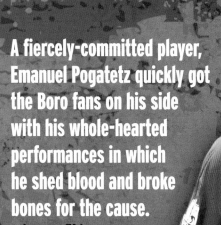

A fiercely-committed player, Emanuel Pogatetz quickly got the Boro fans on his side with his whole-hearted performances in which he shed blood and broke bones for the cause.

EMANUEL POGATETZ

Little was known about the likeable Austrian when he arrived at the Riverside from German side Bayerleverkusen in 2005 as Steve McClaren strengthened his squad for the club's second UEFA Cup campaign. He had played a limited amount of matches for Leverkusen, spending the best part of three years on loan to Aarau, hometown club Grazer AK and Spartak Moscow.

Pogatetz was versatile enough to play in central defence and at full-back. A player of never-say-die commitment, he would throw himself into tackles with relish and soon earned the affectionate nickname "Mad Dog".

During the dramatic journey to Eindhoven, he was unlucky enough to break his nose, jaw and cheekbone in a clash of heads with an opponent in the quarter-final first leg with Basel. That caused him to miss the final, but he was back in action at the start of the 2006/07 season when Gareth Southgate took over from McClaren.

He was given the armband for a spell during the following season and was in the squad that got relegated from the Premier League in 2009. With many of the biggest names leaving the Riverside as the club adjusted to Championship football, Pogatetz stayed on, although his first season in the second tier was badly affected by injuries, including another fractured cheekbone.

He left for Hannover in June 2010 and went on to represent Wolfsburg, West Ham United (on loan) and Nuremberg. Now 32, he is currently playing in the American Major League with Columbus Crew.

George **FRIEND**

Danger Men

![Middlesbrough Football Club 1876 crest](Middlesbrough crest)

Every team have players who can hurt you.

Take a look at the Championship's Danger Men!

BIRMINGHAM CITY
DEMARAI GRAY

The teenager, who scored Blues' Goal of the Season against Wolves, when he ran from his own half, also bagged a hat-trick against Reading. Birmingham-born winger Demarai has the kind of pace and dribbling ability that scares defenders and has already been capped at U20 level by England.

BLACKBURN ROVERS
JORDAN RHODES

Goal machine Jordan grew up with inside knowledge about how to beat goalkeepers. His dad, Andy was a former goalkeeper and was goalkeeping coach at Ipswich Town, where Jordan developed as a youngster. Following a trio of loans, he came to life at Huddersfield with 73 goals in 124 games and since becoming Blackburn's record signing has more than matched that tally.

BOLTON WANDERERS
EMILE HESKEY

Emile Heskey won't score too many goals this season, but whenever a side face the Trotters, the talk in the dressing room will be about how to detect Emile. The veteran England striker is as good a target man as there is. Big and strong Heskey holds the ball up brilliantly and has the experience of over 60 games for England and seven major trophies won with Leicester and Liverpool.

BRENTFORD
JOTA

The Spanish midfielder won Brentford's 'Outstanding Moment of the Season' award, for his winner in the derby with Fulham and was nominated for the Bees' 2014 Mitre Goal of the Year award for his strike against Cardiff City. Technically gifted, Jota played for Real Madrid's 'B' team three years ago.

BRIGHTON & HOVE ALBION
KAZENGA LUALUA

The scorer of Albion's first goal of the season, Kazenga LuaLua is an exciting player, who on his day can cause havoc in opposing defences with his power and trickery. He also struck a cracker against Ipswich Town in an early-season encounter. Having come through the ranks at Newcastle United, Kazenga has now played over 100 games for the Seagulls.

BRISTOL CITY
JONATHAN KODJIA

Last season's French Ligue 2 Player of the Year arrived at Ashton Gate in the summer. The pacey Ivorian striker scored 15 goals in 29 games last season, firing Angers to promotion to the top flight in France. Kodjia wasted no time in showing he had not left his goal touch across the Channel, marking his home debut with a goal against Brentford and bagging another against Burnley before the end of August.

BURNLEY
ANDRE GRAY

Burnley smashed their transfer record to buy Andre Gray from Brentford, for a reported £9m fee. After bagging 18 goals for the Bees last season, Gray scored in the first two matches of his season, including one against newly promoted Bristol City, who wanted to sign him, but Burnley stepped in to snap him up and will look to the former Luton Town man to fire them straight back into the top flight.

CARDIFF CITY
KENWYNE JONES

The spectacular sight of a Kenwyne Jones celebration somersault is something all Bluebirds fans love to see. The tall Trinidadian was once described as the most dangerous player in the game in the air by John Terry and certainly, on his day, no one can keep up with Kenwyne.

CHARLTON ATHLETIC
SIMON MAKIENOK

You cannot miss Makienok, standing 6'7" with his blond ponytail! He has a real physical presence. Not only do his knock-downs put the ball in the danger area for the Addicks attackers, but he is more than useful in his own box too, defending set-pieces. The Dane is a vital player for the men from the Valley.

DERBY COUNTY
TOM INCE

Eleven goals in 18 games on loan last season persuaded the Rams to pay Hull City a reported £4.75m for the son of former England midfielder Paul. Tom is fast, two-footed, tricky and draws people to the ball, before releasing it at just the right moment. He could be the man to take Derby County to the top.

FULHAM
ROSS McCORMACK

Scotland international McCormack cost the Whites £11m in July 2014, an astonishing fee for a newly-relegated club. He proved his worth by netting 19 goals in 50 appearances. An impressive stat, given that he does not always play as an out-and-out striker. His all-round play often means that he is employed in a deeper role, where he is more involved in the game. If Fulham are to do well, McCormack will be a main man.

HUDDERSFIELD TOWN
NAHKI WELLS

Bermuda international Nahki Wells became the Terriers' record signing when he moved from Bradford City. He smashed 25 goals for City in 2012/13, which included strikes in the play-off final and the Capital One Cup semi-final against Villa. Nahki notched 14 goals last season in his first full campaign with Huddersfield and with his pace and persistence, he will always spell danger for the opposition.

IPSWICH TOWN
DARYL MURPHY

Daryl did so well last season he was not so much a Tractor Boy, but a combine harvester, the way he scythed through defences, scoring 27 goals. The Republic of Ireland international hit the form of his life, confidently scoring all kinds of goals for the Portman Road outfit.

MK DONS
DIEGO POYET

The 20-year-old son of Gus Poyet, England U20 international midfielder Diego made five Europa League appearances for West Ham this season, before joining MK Dons. His passing ability and footballing philosophy fits snugly into the Dons' renowned possession game. Poyet was Charlton's Young Player of the Year the season before last, despite not debuting until January of that campaign.

HULL CITY
MOSES ODUBAJO

Looking to bounce straight back to the top flight, the Tigers invested a reported £3.5m to capture England U20 Moses Odubajo from Brentford. He missed just one game last season as the Bees just missed out on promotion, losing in the play-off semi-final. A right-winger or right-back, Moses spent four years with Leyton Orient, winning the O's Goal of the Season in 2011/12 and was voted their Young Player of the Year the following season.

LEEDS UNITED
MIRCO ANTENUCCI

The veteran Italian striker has represented nine clubs in his own country, including Torino, with whom he won promotion to Serie 'A' in 2011/12. Muscular and mobile, Mirco hit double figures for Leeds last season and scored a stunner against Burnley to start the current campaign with a bang.

NOTTINGHAM FOREST
BRITT ASSOMBALONGA

Britt Assombalonga will not be fit until the second half of the season, but he could be the man to fire Forest to promotion, if they can keep themselves in the running until then. Britt had scored 15 times before his injury in February, a tally that gives him over 50 in the last three years.

PRESTON NORTH END
DANIEL JOHNSON

aniel's eight goals in the second half of last
eason, after joining in January, helped North End
promotion. Having earlier scored three times
n loan to Oldham, Jamaican-born Johnson was
double figures for the season and after getting
f to a good start with the first home goal at
eepdale this season, he will hope to reach that
rget again.

QUEENS PARK RANGERS
CHARLIE AUSTIN

arclays Premier League Player of the Month for
ecember 2014, Charlie was called up by England,
though he still awaits his first cap. QPR fans
ere relieved he did not move on in the transfer
indow, as many clubs were understandably keen
n signing a player who has scored well over 100
oals for QPR, Burnley and Swindon after making
s name in non-league football.

READING
OLA JOHN

John signed for the Royals on a season-long loan
in the summer from Benfica. He is a very talented
forward with power, pace, the ability to beat his man,
deliver quality balls into the box and also has an eye
for goal himself. With all these attributes, Ola should
help ensure Reading are a potent offensive force
this campaign.

ROTHERHAM UNITED
JORDAN BOWERY

Bowery impressed so much as a youngster at
Chesterfield that Aston Villa spent £500,000 on him
when he was only 21. Jordan is an impact player, with
28 of his 36 appearances last term coming off the
bench, but a clue to his quality was that two of his
five goals came against teams subsequently promoted
to the Barclays Premier League.

SHEFFIELD WEDNESDAY
MARCO MATIAS

Matias' early-season goal at Leeds marked him
out as a special player. The way he lobbed the
ball over Liam Cooper before applying the most
spectacular finish, was pure quality. Last season
he scored 17 goals in 33 games in the Portuguese
top flight for CD Nacional, while home fans saw
his first goal at Hillsborough come against
Middlesbrough in August.

WOLVERHAMPTON WANDERERS
BENIK AFOBE

Goals, goals, goals are what Afobe is all about.
He struck three times in the first four games of
this season after scoring 32 last term, 13 of them
after his move to Molineux from MK Dons. The
22-year-old came through the ranks at Arsenal and
the England U21 international was reportedly the
subject of a £12m bid from Norwich City in August.

What ball?

There are too many footballs in these action shots!

Can you figure out which balls are real?

ANSWERS ON PAGE 62

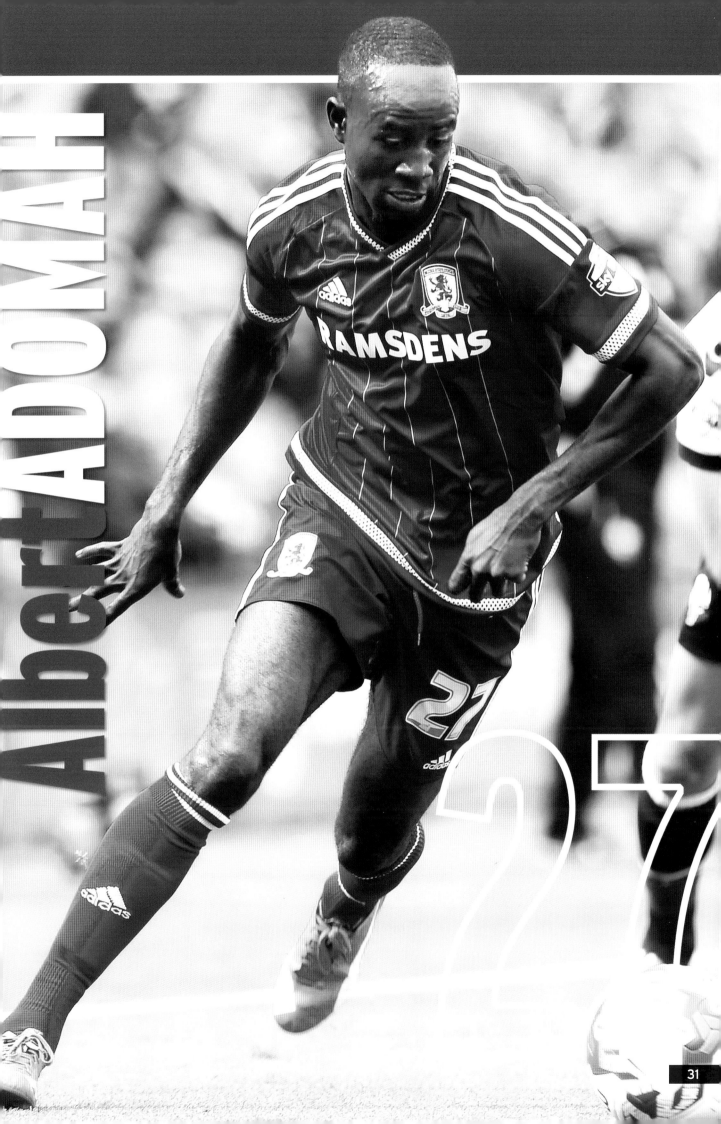

Albert ADOMAH

2016
Predictions

OUR PREDICTION FOR ALSO PROMOTED TO THE BARCLAYS PREMIER LEAGUE:

Burnley & Ipswich Town

YOUR PREDICTION:

OUR PREDICTION FOR SKY BET CHAMPIONSHIP WINNERS:

Boro

YOUR PREDICTION:

OUR PREDICTION FOR SKY BET CHAMPIONSHIP BOTTOM THREE:

Brentford, Preston and Rotherham

YOUR PREDICTION:

Championship

OUR PREDICTION FOR BARCLAYS PREMIER LEAGUE CHAMPIONS:

Chelsea

YOUR PREDICTION:

Premier League

League Cup

OUR PREDICTION FOR LEAGUE CUP WINNERS:

Manchester City

YOUR PREDICTION:

OUR PREDICTION FOR FA CUP WINNERS:

Derby County

YOUR PREDICTION:

OUR PREDICTION FOR BARCLAYS PREMIER LEAGUE RUNNERS-UP:

Arsenal

YOUR PREDICTION:

FA Cup

Adam CLAYTON

8

On the Road

ANSWERS ON PAGE 62

Crowd Pleasers

Can you spot the five British actors hidden in the crowd?

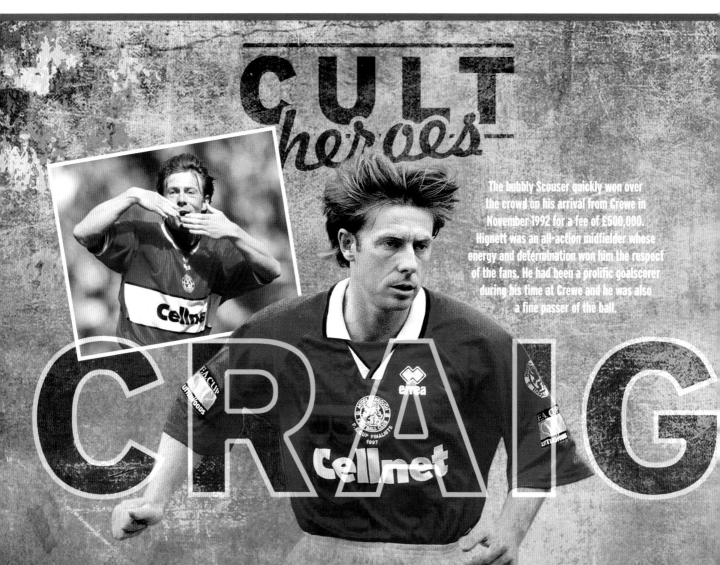

CULT heroes

CRAIG

HIGNETT

The bubbly Scouser quickly won over the crowd on his arrival from Crewe in November 1992 for a fee of £500,000. Hignett was an all-action midfielder whose energy and determination won him the respect of the fans. He had been a prolific goalscorer during his time at Crewe and he was also a fine passer of the ball.

He was signed by Lennie Lawrence during Boro's inaugural season in the new Premier League and it quickly turned into a battle for survival. Although he could not prevent relegation to the First Division, he proved a valuable addition to the squad.

Hignett scored four goals in a Coca-Cola Cup tie with Brighton, becoming the first Boro player to achieve the feat for 15 years, but was in and out of Lawrence's side. When Bryan Robson took over as manager, he became a fringe member of the squad that won the First Division championship and was being touted for sale at one point. But he refused to give up on his Middlesbrough dream and took a pay cut to stay at the club. Hignett formed an instant partnership with Nick Barmby as Boro settled comfortably in the top flight during the 1995/96 season. Fans dubbed them the "Midget Gems".

The goal that will always be remembered came against Chelsea on the opening day of the season in August 1995 as Boro fans took their places at the Riverside Stadium for the first time.

Hignett experienced his second relegation in Middlesbrough colours when Robson's side went down in 1997 following their year of two cup final defeats. He played one final season for the club, signing off in May 1998 with two goals against Oxford United as Boro reclaimed their place in the Premier League at the first attempt.

After a short spell with Aberdeen, he played for Barnsley, Blackburn, Leicester and a host of other clubs before taking his coaching badges and spending some time back at Boro as a youth coach and latterly as assistant head coach.

Here are the nicknames of every Championship Club, can you work out who the team is and then find them in the grid?

```
P H U D D E R S F I E L D T O W N O C N C Q
A R I S E P M M E G T H U H A O A B I B H U
U A E L Y T I C L O T S I R B L W H H E A E
L I P S W I C H T O W N S K M V S G U C R E
A T M G T K B A F R B F N B H E T U L Z L N
Q S Y P E O L U K G N I D A E R R O L P T S
W E T I E B N H R U S T P E O H T R C S O P
B R I G H T O N A N D H O V E A L B I O N A
I O C I D I G R O A L C S I H M U S T S A R
R F F Y V J A D Q R C E J A V P S E Y Q T K
M M F D G W K F O C T I Y T S T K L T U H R
I A I O F M S E G U O H B K A O I D I W L A
N H D D E T I N U S D E E L S N R D G H E N
G G R A N K E M D V A U E N D W O I E W T G
H N A N F C A N Z L F B I S D A Y M R S I E
A I C T J H D R O F T N E R B N D Q S R C R
M T X O L C B O L T O N W A N D E R E R S S
C T Y U Y A D S E N D E W D L E I F F E H S
I O F M W U J Y T N U O C Y B R E D B E X Y
T N P B L A C K B U R N R O V E R S P G I A
Y D E T I N U M A H R E H T O R V I W K O N
      O X M P L O N E S Y C S W B H
```

Name that Team...

1. Robins _____
2. Rovers _____
3. Royals _____
4. Boro _____
5. Cottagers _____
6. Clarets _____
7. Bluebirds _____
8. Blues _____
9. Seagulls _____
10. Terriers _____
11. Bees _____
12. Tigers _____
13. Whites _____
14. Hoops _____
15. The Dons _____
16. Wolves _____
17. Millers _____
18. Owls _____
19. Forest _____
20. Trotters _____
21. Lilywhites _____
22. Tractor Boys _____
23. Addicks _____
24. Rams _____

Player of the Year
Grant Leadbitter

Since his arrival on Teesside more than three years ago, Grant Leadbitter has been a model professional.

The midfielder wins the respect of his teammates through the consistent quality of his performances and is a natural leader on the field.

It came as no surprise when Leadbitter was named Player of the Year for the second time in 2014/15. He scored a career-best 11 goals from the middle of the park and hardly missed a game in an exciting season of league and cup achievement.

He was also Boro captain in the absence of Jonathan Woodgate and inspired his colleagues through his never-say-die attitude and 100 per cent commitment in both matches and training.

Tony Mowbray snapped him up from Ipswich in summer 2012 following completion of his three-year contract at Portman Road. Leadbitter had moved to East Anglia after starting his career with Sunderland, the club he supported as a boy. He made more than 100 appearances for the Black Cats, leaving the Stadium of Light to team up with his former Sunderland manager, Mick McCarthy, at Ipswich.

His dream of helping them into the Premier League never materialised, and Mowbray was delighted to bring him back to the North East to become the lynchpin of his midfield. Leadbitter has the job of protecting the defence but has always had the knack of weighing in with vital goals.

He was particularly effective from the penalty spot last season and was a driving force for the team on and off the field. No-one was more disappointed when Boro lost out to Norwich in the Championship play-off final at Wembley, but Leadbitter is relishing the challenge of leading a successful promotion campaign this season.

Mega Pixels

Can you identify these Boro stars?

1

3

2

Team Talk

YANIC WILDSCHUT

Pizza? Shoarma

Game? Call of Duty

Film? Blood Diamond

Actor? Tom Cruise

Actress? Megan Fox

Animal? Dog

Song? Born Sinner, J Cole

Colour? Grey

Place? No Place Bike (Amsterdam)

Sweets? I don't like sweets – I only eat fruit

Who is the toughest player you've played against? Ryan Fredericks

What has been the best moment of your career? Playing for Holland U21

Who do you most admire in football? The Brazilian Ronaldo

Have you got any pre-match superstitions? No

What's your career advice for young talent out there? Work hard, make the most of your career. You'll be sorry in the end if you didn't give it your all

What is your most annoying habit? Laziness

What would your theme tune be? The Mighty Boro are Going Up

What is the funniest thing that has happened to you recently? Just some dressing-room banter, but we keep that private!

If you were on an island and could only bring three things, what would you bring? Food, bed and Megan Fox

Name three people, alive or dead, who you'd invite to your fantasy dinner party? Megan Fox, the Brazilian Ronaldo and Ryan Leslie

What's the most interesting thing we don't know about you? I can dance salsa and bachata

ADAM FORSHAW

FAVOURITES

Pizza? Ham & pineapple
Film? Southpaw
Actress? Cameron Diaz
Place? Florida
Song? Thinking Out Loud, Ed Sheeran
Game? Golf
Actor? Jim Carey
Animal? Dog
Sweets? Haribo
Colour? Red

Who is the toughest player you have played against? Frank Lampard

What has been the best moment of your career? Playing in the Premier League

What's your career advice for young talent out there? Hard work beats talent

If you were on an island and could only bring three things, what would you bring? Phone, football and the missus

Name three people, alive or dead, who you'd invite to your fantasy dinner party? Steven Gerrard, Ed Sheeran and Cheryl Cole

What's the most interesting thing we don't know about you? I had a heart operation when I was 17 and had to decide whether to continue with football or not

DAMIA

FAVOURITES

Pizza? Four cheese
Film? Pulp Fiction
Actress? Meryl Streep
Place? Cadagues, Spain
Colour? Blue
Game? Anything extreme
Actor? Christopher Waltz
Animal? Dog
Sweets? Any
Song? Dock of the Bay, Otis Reading

Who do you most admire in football? Carles Puyol, Sylvinho

Have you got any pre-match superstitions? No, I have some routines

What's your career advice for young talent out there? Always be a team player

What is your most annoying habit? Using my mobile phone too much

If you were on an island and could only bring three things, what would you bring? Surfboard, sun cream and a fridge with plenty of drinks

Who would you invite to your fantasy dinner party? Nelson Mandela and Will Smith

What's the most interesting thing we don't know about you? I'm an American classic car fanatic

David HUGENT

Design
A NEW KIT

Puzzle IT OUT

CAREER WATCH

Work out the missing teams in George Friend's career.

2005-2008	Exeter City
2008-2010	
2010-2012	
2012-	Middlesbrough

Who are yer?

Three Boro players are mixed up in this pictur

DERBY DAY

Can you match each team to their rival?

1

2

3

4

HOMELANDS

Match the player to their home country

The Netherlands	Kike
Diego Fabbrini	Australia
Spain	Yanic Wildschut
Rhys Williams	Ghana
Czech Republic	Albert Adomah
Tomas Kalas	Italy

CULT *heroes*

GIANLUCA FESTA

Another player who stayed loyal to the club following relegation was Gianluca Festa, a charismatic Sardinian who became a firm crowd favourite at the Riverside. The accomplished defender was the perfect ambassador for overseas players during his five years on Teesside.

He arrived in England in January 1997, midway through one of the most dramatic seasons in Boro's history. He had played at the Riverside a year earlier in Willie Maddren's testimonial match, as an Inter Milan player.

Festa left the San Siro to try to help Boro stay in the Premier League, arriving in the same week as Vladimir Kinder. He immediately stood out with his passionate displays, with powerful tackles and commanding headers that became his trademark.

He was unable to prevent Boro going down that season and also shared in the heartbreak of losing the 1997 League Cup and FA Cup finals. Festa was outstanding the following season as Bryan Robson's side immediately bounced back to the top flight. He also played in his third Wembley final in just 12 months when he appeared against Chelsea in the 1998 Coca-Cola Cup final, a game Boro lost 2-0.

The Italian international helped Boro to stabilise back in the Premier League in 1998/99 as they achieved a ninth-placed finish, sharing centre-back duties with Gary Pallister and Steve Vickers. He could also play at full-back in midfield when the need arose.

Festa continued to be a regular during Robson's reign but found himself out of favour when Steve McClaren took over in 2001. He moved back to Sardinia with Cagliari, where he also had a spell in management.

The Team
behind the team

MIDDLESBROUGH
FOOTBALL CLUB
1876

AITOR KARANKA

Aitor Karanka was appointed as Boro's Head Coach in November 2013, becoming the club's first foreigner to take charge of team affairs. His success in guiding the team to the Championship play-off final in May 2015 was rewarded in the shape of a new four-year contract last summer.

A proud Basque, Karanka spent most of his playing career in his native Spain with two clubs, Athletic Bilbao and Real Madrid. The centre-back featured in 100 league matches for Bilbao before joining his German-born manager Jupp Heynckes at Real Madrid.

He won seven major titles with Real, including the Champions League in 2000, before returning to Bilbao and helping them qualify for the UEFA Cup. In 2006, he switched to Major League Soccer in the United States with Colorado Rapids.

In his only season with Colorado, he helped his team win the Western Conference play-off final. Karanka won one senior cap with Spain.

At the end of his playing career, he turned to coaching and worked with the junior Spanish national sides. In June 2010, he was appointed assistant manager to Jose Mourinho at Real Madrid. He spent three years in the post, during which time Real won the La Liga title in 2011/12.

After arriving at Boro, Karanka gradually undertook an overhaul of the squad and introduced new training methods. The 2014/15 season saw his team in the leading positions all season, with a thrilling victory over Manchester City in the FA Cup and a dramatic penalty shootout defeat to Liverpool in the Capital One Cup.

Boro just missed out at the final hurdle, losing the play-off final to Norwich at Wembley.

STEVE AGNEW

Agnew took over as Assistant Head Coach a year ago following a highly successful spell with Hull City, where he was right-hand man to Steve Bruce as the Tigers won promotion to the Premier League and reached the 2014 FA Cup final.

It's the second time he has been on the Boro coaching staff, having been second-team manager and Academy coach during his first spell at Rockliffe Park.

As a player, he represented Barnsley, Blackburn, Portsmouth, Leicester, Sunderland and York City. His coaching career has also included spells at Leeds and Hartlepool.

LEO PERCOVICH

Percovich is Goalkeeper Coach at Boro and works closely with Aitor Karanka, who he met playing Major League Soccer in the USA.

He is a former Uruguayan international goalkeeper who represented Nacional, where he was a Copa Libertadores and Uruguayan First Division winner, Atlético Mineiro, Guaraní FC, Fluminense FC, Alianza de Lima and Racing de Ferrol. He won six caps for Uruguay.

He has previously coached at Stuttgart, Pachuca, Cruzeiro, Valencia, Real Madrid, Colorado Rapids, Chivas USA, Toronto FC and most recently Chicago, as well as the Brazil, France and Uruguay national teams.

CARLOS CACHADA

Cachada is Fitness Assistant who has previous experience in Turkey and with Portuguese clubs Uniao De Leiria and Vitoria Setubal.

He joined Boro upon the arrival of Spanish Head Coach Aitor Karanka in November 2013.

IVAN PEREZ MUNOZ

The First Team Coach formerly played for Real Madrid and joined Aitor Karanka's coaching staff during summer 2014.

His La Liga career included spells with Real and Deportivo, and he also represented Spain at all levels up to U23.

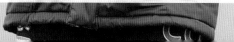

The Writing's on the Wall

Decorate the wall and show your love for Boro!

Diego FABBRINI

31

Test Yourself on 2015
The Championship

01

BIRMINGHAM CITY

What was Blues' highest home attendance last season?

02

BLACKBURN ROVERS

Who was Blackburn's top League goal scorer last season?

03

BOLTON WANDERERS

Who was Bolton's first signing this summer?

04

BRENTFORD

The Bees finished fifth last season and made it to the play-offs. But who were they defeated by in the semi-finals?

05

BRIGHTON & HOVE ALBION

The Seagulls are the most southern team in the Championship. True or false?

08

CARDIFF CITY

Cardiff is the only Welsh team in the Championship. True or false?

06

BRISTOL CITY

Bristol City were promoted as champions this season, how many points did they top the League One table with?

07

BURNLEY

Who scored the Clarets' first goal of the 2015/16 season?

09

CHARLTON ATHLETIC

Which shot stopper is wearing the No.1 jersey for the Addicks this season?

10

DERBY COUNTY

Derby got a new manager this season to replace Steve McClaren. Who is he?

11

FULHAM

Name the Fulham player who scored two hat-tricks last season!

12

HUDDERSFIELD TOWN

Who made the most appearances in total for the Terriers' last season?

13

HULL CITY

Who was Hull City's £1.3m summer signing from Chesterfield this season?

14

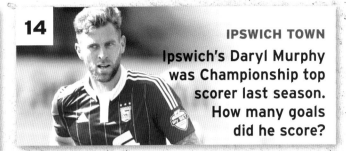

IPSWICH TOWN
Ipswich's Daryl Murphy was Championship top scorer last season. How many goals did he score?

15

LEEDS UNITED

Uwe Rosler is Leeds' new manager this season. Who did he replace?

16

MK DONS
Who is captaining MK Dons this season?

17

NOTTINGHAM FOREST
A Forest player received the Player of the Month award in February 2015. Who was he?

18

PRESTON NORTH END
What colour is the Lilywhites' away kit this season?

19

QUEENS PARK RANGERS

Who was first to sign for the Hoops this summer on a free transfer from Bristol City?

20

READING
Who was Reading's first League win of the 2015/16 season against?

21

ROTHERHAM UNITED
Which hot shot is wearing the No.9 jersey for the Millers this season?

23

WOLVERHAMPTON WANDERERS

Wolves have a new sponsor this season. Who is it?

22

SHEFFIELD WEDNESDAY
Who will the Owls play in their last game of 2015?

GEORGE FRIEND

FAVOURITES

Pizza? Meat

Film? Batman

Actress? Blake Lively

Sweets? Don't eat them!

Song? We Built This City, Starship

Place? Los Angeles – Hermosa Beach

Game? Volleyball

Actor? Leo DiCaprio

Animal? Cow

Colour? Blue

Who is the toughest player you've played against?
David Silva

What has been the best moment of your career?
Playing in the Premier League at Old Trafford

Who do you most admire in football?
Paolo Maldini

Have you got any pre-match superstitions? No

What's your career advice for young talent out there?
Play every match as if it's at Wembley

What is your most annoying habit?
I bite my nails

What would your theme tune be?
The theme tune from Friends

What is the funniest thing that has happened to you recently?
Can't think of anything

If you were on an island and could only bring three things, what would you bring?
My wife, my daughter and a surfboard

Name three people, alive or dead, who you'd invite to your fantasy dinner party?
Jesus, Father Christmas and Boris Johnson

What's the most interesting thing we don't know about you?
I play the drums and ukulele

JONATHAN WOODGATE

Who is the toughest player you've played against? Alan Shearer

What has been the best moment of your career? My England and Boro debuts

Who do you most admire in football? Gary Neville

Have you got any pre-match superstitions? I put my shirt on straight away

What's your career advice for young talent out there? Work as hard as you can every day

What is your most annoying habit? Not making the bed

What would your theme tune be? Handjive (from the film Grease)

What is the funniest thing that has happened to you recently? Can't think of anything

If you were on an island and could only bring three things, what would you bring? My son, my wife and my mobile phone

Name three people, alive or dead, who you'd invite to your fantasy dinner party? My father, Mike Tyson, Bobby Robson and Napoleon

KIKE

9

CULT heroes

Colin Todd paid £500,000 for the much-travelled John Hendrie in July 1990, and it was money well spent. The Scot's direct attacking style was exciting to watch and he scored vital goals at pivotal moments in his Boro career.

Soon after his arrival, he scored one of the greatest goals ever seen. Picking up the ball outside his own box, he ran half the length of the pitch before shooting into Millwall's net.

Hendrie's rise to cult status picked up speed when Todd's successor, Lennie Lawrence, brought him in from the wing to play as a central striker. The goals started to flow but the switch came too late to save Boro from relegation.

His partnership with Paul Wilkinson continued to flourish, however, his speed and tricky skills being the perfect foil for Wilkinson's aerial ability. He was named in the Professional Footballers' Association team of the season in 1993/94 after starting the campaign in explosive scoring fashion.

Hendrie's good form continued during Bryan Robson's first season in charge and he scored both goals in a 2-1 win over Luton that all but ensured promotion and the First Division championship in the last match at Ayresome Park in April 1995.

Injuries affected him as the club moved into their new home at the Riverside and he found it difficult to win a place following the arrival of big names such as Nick Barmby, Juninho and Fabrizio Ravanelli.

He left the club for Barnsley in 1996 and renewed his partnership with Wilkinson, helping the Tykes to promotion to the top flight for the first time in their history and also winning their player of the year award.

Hendrie had a brief spell as manager of Barnsley before forging a new career as a sports consultant. He is also a matchday host at the Riverside.

John Hendrie

Challenge 16

We've set you a huge challenge for the new year!

EVERY MONTH THERE ARE TWO TASKS TO COMPLETE

JANUARY

- ☐ Do **25** keepy-uppies.
- ☐ Come up with a new Boro chant!

FEBRUARY

- ☐ Take a selfie at a Championship Stadium.
- ☐ LEARN A NEW TRICK **Around the world**

MARCH

- ☐ **NUTMEG** your best mate!
- ☒ Get an autograph from a Boro star player.

- ☐ Do **50** keepy-uppies.
- ☐ Take a selfie with a Boro star.

APRIL

MAY

- ☐ WORK ON YOUR FITNESS **Run 1 mile!**
- ☐ **Lob the keeper**

JUNE

- [ ] **LEARN A NEW TRICK**
  Catch the ball on the back your neck!

- [ ] Do your bit for charity - set up a sponsored event with your mates.

JULY

- [ ] **KEEPY-UPPY CHALLENGE**
  10 with a... **tennis ball!**

- [ ] **WORK ON YOUR FITNESS**
  Run 3 mile!

AUGUST

- [ ] Take a selfie with a Boro legend.

- [ ] Do **75** keepy-uppies.

SEPTEMBER

- [ ] **KEEPY-UPPY CHALLENGE**
  10 on your... **head!**

- [ ] Try out for your school footie team.

OCTOBER

- [ ] **Shake Roary the Lion's hand.**

- [ ] Take a selfie with **Aitor Karanka**

NOVEMBER

- [x] **WORK ON YOUR FITNESS**
  Run 5 mile!

- [x] Blast a penalty in off the underside of the crossbar.

DECEMBER

- [x] Do **100** keepy-uppies.

- [x] Start a chant at the match.

Answers

PAGE 18 · TEST YOURSELF ON 2015, MIDDLESBROUGH FC

1. Patrick Bamford, 17 goals, 2. Albert Adomah, 3. Alex Baptiste,
4. January, 5. Grant Leadbitter, Kike and Albert Adomah, 6. Uruguay,
7. Michael Agazzi, 8. Brighton & Hove Albion, 9. Stewart Downing,
10. Mustapha Carayol, 11. Sheffield Wednesday, 12. Huddersfield Town,
13. Diego Fabbrini, 14. 12, 15. MK Dons

PAGE 20 · SPOT THE DIFFERENCE ⟶

PAGE 30 · WHAT BALL

Picture A - Ball 7, Picture B - Ball 3

PAGE 35 · ON THE ROAD

1. Cardiff City, 2. Rotherham United, 3. Leeds United,
4. Brighton & Hove Albion, 5. Bolton Wanderers,
6. Derby County, 7. Burnley, 8. Birmingham City, 9. MK Dons

PAGE 36 · CROWD PLEASERS

PAGE 42 · MEGA PIXELS

1. Stewart Downing, 2. George Friend, 3. Grant Leadbitter,
4. Diego Fabbrini, 5. Adam Clayton, 6. Bradley Fewster,
7. Kike, 8. Emilio Nsue, 9. Cristhian Stuani

PAGE 48 · PUZZLE IT OUT

CAREER WATCH

2008–2010: Wolverhampton Wanderers,
2010–2012: Doncaster Rovers

DERBY DAY

1. Derby County - Nottingham Forest,
2. Brighton & Hove Albion - Crystal Palace,
3. Ipswich Town - Norwich City,
4. Wolverhampton Wanderers - West Bromwich Albion

WHO ARE YER?

Cristhian Stuani, David Nugent and Adam Clayton

HOMELANDS

Kike - Spain, Rhys Williams - Australia, Diego Fabbrini - Italy,
Yanic Wildschut - The Netherlands, Albert Adomah - Ghana,
Tomas Kalas - Czech Republic

PAGE 39 · NAME THAT TEAM

1. Robins - Bristol City, 2. Rovers - Blackburn Rovers,
3. Royals - Reading, 4. Boro - Middlesbrough,
5. Cottagers - Fulham, 6. Clarets - Burnley, 7. Bluebirds - Cardiff City,
8. Blues - Birmingham City, 9. Seagulls - Brighton and Hove Albion,
10. Terriers - Huddersfield Town, 11. Bees - Brentford,
12. Tigers - Hull City, 13. Whites - Leeds United,
14. Hoops - Queens Park Rangers, 15. The Dons - MK Dons,
16. Wolves - Wolverhampton Wanderers,
7. Millers - Rotherham United, 18. Owls - Sheffield Wednesday
19. Forest - Nottingham Forest, 20. Trotters - Bolton Wanderers
21. Lilywhites - Preston North End, 22. Tractor Boys - Ipswich Town
23. Addicks - Charlton Athletic, 24. Rams - Derby County

PAGE 54 · TEST YOURSELF ON 2015, THE CHAMPIONSHIP

1. 28,438 (v West Bromwich Albion, FA Cup 4th round,
24 January 2015), 2. Jordan Rhodes with 21 League goals,
3. Ben Amos, 4. Middlesbrough, 5. True, 6. 99, 7. Sam Vokes,
8. True, 9. Stephen Henderson, 10. Paul Clement,
11. Ross McCormack, 12. Conor Coady with 48 appearances,
13. Sam Clucas, 14. 27, 15. Neil Redfearn, 16. Dean Lewington,
17. Henri Lansbury, 18. Yellow and blue, 19. Jay Emmanuel-Thomas,
20. Brentford, 21. Danny Ward, 22. Middlesbrough, 23. Silverbug